"Don't Let Your Emotions Run Your Life for ...... l facilitating meaningful dialogue between parents, caregivers, family members, and children for explaining and exploring emotions. The workbook discusses a variety of emotions using language geared towards children, and provides concrete examples of what emotions 'look' like while giving children the tools needed to identify and communicate their emotional experiences. The exercises are designed to teach the child using easily understandable concepts and 'kid friendly,' concrete exercises to help guide them through each concept. The activities are designed to facilitate an enriched learning experience, uniquely applicable to each child. The workbook is well written, and the authors are clearly compassionate and dedicated to helping children recognize their emotions and how those emotions impact the world around them."

> —**Julie A. Vandermay, PsyD, MA**, forensic neuropsychology resident at Natalis Counseling & Psychology Solutions

"Don't Let Your Emotions Run Your Life for Kids effectively conveys useful information about the challenging emotions children face, and ways for kids to deal with them in language far more accessible than most material available on these topics. As a plus, parents who assist their children in the useful exercises provided in the book may well find themselves picking up helpful tips for managing *their* own emotions as well!"

> —**Mark Carlson-Ghost, PhD**, associate professor at the Minnesota School of Professional Psychology at Argosy University-Twin Cities Campus

"Very well done! I do dialectical behavior therapy (DBT) with adults, and I could easily see the transition to kid-friendly language and concepts without losing any information. I think kids will be able to dive into these concepts quickly and easily. I can see this as being very helpful in a variety of settings."

> —**Reena Pathak, PsyD**, licensed psychologist

"Don't Let Your Emotions Run Your Life for Kids is a great resource for children in that it provides clear explanations to help them gain understanding about what emotions are and why we have them, and it and contains both fun and educational activities to assist them in learning how to express emotions more effectively. Parents will also benefit from this workbook because it provides them with clear, straightforward, age-appropriate language they can use to talk to their children about feelings in a manner that will facilitate an open dialogue and enhance the parent-child relationship."

> —**Ilyssa Siegel, PsyD**, mental health practitioner at an addiction treatment center

"Don't Let Your Emotions Run Your Life for Kids provides an easy-to-understand and effective set of tools to help kids navigate the complexities of emotions they may be struggling with. The tools help kids learn to understand, manage, and express their thoughts and feelings in ways that will help enhance their lives and reduce turmoil they might otherwise experience. These simple yet powerful tools draw from modern-day clinical methods which are helpful in reducing distress and increasing one's ability to interact with others in meaningful ways."

> —**Robert Hoppe, PsyD**, licensed psychologist

"This workbook provides an excellent tool for professionals and parents alike to skillfully empower children to learn to manage difficult emotions through practical and engaging examples and activities."

> —**Megan Thumann, PsyD**, licensed psychologist and mother of four boys

Don't Let Your Emotions Run Your Life for Kids

A DBT-Based Skills Workbook to Help Children Manage Mood Swings, Control Angry Outbursts, and Get Along with Others

JENNIFER J. SOLIN, PsyD

CHRISTINA L. KRESS, MSW

Instant Help Books

An Imprint of New Harbinger Publications, Inc.

Publisher's Note

Distributed in Canada by Raincoast Books

Copyright © 2017 by Jennifer Jean Solin and Christina L. Kress
             Instant Help Books
             An imprint of New Harbinger Publications, Inc.
             5674 Shattuck Avenue
             Oakland, CA 94609
             www.newharbinger.com

INSTANT HELP, the Clock Logo, and NEW HARBINGER are trademarks of New Harbinger Publications, Inc.

Cover photo is for illustrative purposes only

Cover design by Amy Shoup

Acquired by Elizabeth Hollis Hansen

Edited by Karen Schader

Library of Congress Cataloging-in-Publication Data on file

Printed in the United States of America

23   22

15   14   13   12   11   10   9

FSC
www.fsc.org
MIX
Paper from
responsible sources
FSC® C011935

Contents

Section 3: Working with Your Feelings

Section 4: Creating Your Skills Toolbox

Section 5: Taking Your Tools on the Road

Section 6: Values and Goals

A Note to Parents

Welcome to *Don't Let Your Emotions Run Your Life for Kids*. We are pleased you have chosen this workbook and hope these activities can help you and your child manage your child's out-of-control feelings.

The activities in this book are a compilation of original ideas based on over twelve years of experience working with young children, adolescents, and adults, using cognitive behavioral therapy (CBT), dialectical behavior therapy (DBT), and play-therapy techniques. CBT is a therapy that examines the connection between thoughts and behaviors and was originally developed by Dr. Aaron Beck in 1960. DBT is a treatment approach researched and developed by Dr. Marsha Linehan that is used with adults and adolescents who struggle with experiencing intense feelings.

We paid careful attention to adapting skills in a way that would allow them to be used as hands-on activities. Though the specific activities in this workbook have not been empirically validated, we have found them extremely useful in helping us begin conversations about intense emotions and encouraging children to learn coping skills as well as to use them more often and more effectively.

You may notice that some activities closely resemble others. This is intentional, since school-age children learn best through repeated exposure to, and behavioral rehearsal of, the same concepts presented in slightly different ways.

Children will require some adult direction with each activity in order to gain the most from the material. Feelings can be scary and confusing for young children, and having an adult help them understand thoughts, feelings, and behaviors is very important. A child who is experiencing intense feelings may not be able to remember what coping skills could be useful. Several times throughout the book we remind readers to practice their skills. We are encouraging you and your child to rehearse applying these coping skills together so that you can guide your child through experiencing intense feelings when they emerge. This practice presents a perfect opportunity for you to gently remind your child about the skills learned from this book. Research among adults who actively practice learned coping skills has demonstrated that those who practice often see the most improvement in their daily living. Practice can include modeling by adults, behavioral rehearsal, role-plays, and praise provided to the child.

The printed book is divided into six sections, and a seventh section is available at http://www.newharbinger.com/38594. Online, you'll also find appendices that explain each section, provide important takeaways, and suggest ways to help your child gain the most from the activities. In addition, you'll find downloadable content that relates to activities in the printed book and additional activities to enrich your child's skill building.

Section 1

Mindfulness Activities

Have you ever noticed that your brain and your body sometimes seem to be in two different places? Your body might be at school, but your brain and your mind are thinking about home. You might be sitting at the dinner table talking with your parents, but your mind is thinking about the argument you had with your friend at recess earlier in the day. When this happens it can be difficult for you to focus. In this section you are going to learn about your mind and how to help it focus.

Your mind is like a muscle. If you practice focusing your mind, it will become stronger and you will notice that you are able to focus more on things that you want to focus on. We call this being mindful.

Good luck as you get started, and remember that these things take practice. It might be a little challenging at first, but you can do it!

You Have Different Types of Thoughts

For You to Know

Your mind produces different types of thoughts. Learning to know the difference between helpful and unhelpful thoughts can help you change your thoughts so that they can be more helpful.

Your mind creates thoughts, feelings, and ways of thinking about the world. It has three main areas: one that creates thoughts and urges out of feelings, one that creates thoughts and urges out of the facts you see around you, and one that mixes the two together. Take a minute to look at the picture below to see the different areas.

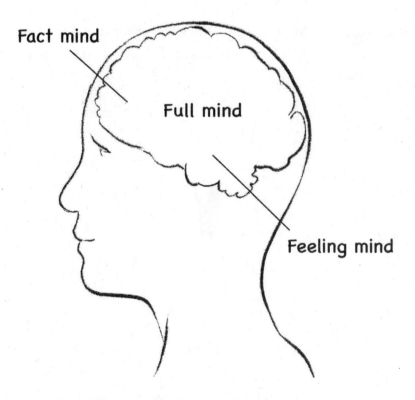

Fact mind

Full mind

Feeling mind

Don't Let Your Emotions Run Your Life for Kids

The fact area of your mind creates thoughts that focus only on the task that needs to be done and the things it can observe. For example, your fact mind can look out the window and see that the thermometer says thirty degrees. When it's thirty degrees outside, your thoughts tell you to wear a jacket. This is a helpful thought because it keeps us safe.

The feeling mind area creates thoughts that focus only on feelings, moods, and getting what you want. Your feeling mind is where your wants and opinions come from. For example, Daniel looks out the window, sees the thermometer, knows it's cold and thinks, *Yeah! I get to wear my new jacket. I want to go outside and play.* Daniel is mixing together facts and his feelings to make a helpful decision. Christopher might look out the same window, see the thermometer, know it's cold, and think, *Yuck! I hate my new jacket. I don't want to go outside. I'd rather go back to bed.* Daniel and Christopher both know it's cold, but they have different wants and opinions about wearing their jackets. These different opinions come from Daniel's and Christopher's distinct feeling minds.

Your full mind includes both the facts and your feelings and is where they come together to help you make helpful decisions. In the example above, when Daniel looked out the window and saw it was cold (fact mind), his thought about needing to wear a jacket in order to be safe was a helpful thought—it helped him be able to go outside and have fun. For Christopher, his thought about not liking his jacket and not wanting to go outside because of it stopped him from having fun.

For You to Do

Read the example below and circle the helpful thoughts. Do you notice helpful thoughts like these throughout your day? Try to catch yourself having helpful thoughts whenever you can. Noticing helpful thoughts makes it easier to choose helpful behaviors.

Example: You are playing your favorite video game, and your parent tells you it's time for dinner. You notice these thoughts:

- I want to keep playing my game.

- They never let me finish my game.

- I'm a little hungry.

- I can save my game and play later.

- I don't want to stop my game right now.

Think of the helpful thoughts you circled, and write down why you think they are helpful thoughts.

_____

_____

_____

Why do you think the unhelpful thoughts might get in the way?

_____

_____

_____

Facts and Feelings Are Not the Same

For You to Know

Reviewing the facts of a situation can help us figure out what can change and what is out of our control. The facts of a situation are often out of our control, but we do have some control over how we feel about it.

Frankie Fact and Fiona Feeling are cousins who both work in your mind. When they work together, they create thoughts and decisions that come from your full mind. When they don't get along or work together, it can cause problems!

Let's start by getting to know Frankie Fact. Frankie loves to focus only on things that are proven facts, things that are the same for everyone, like science and math. He has some favorite ways of thinking. For example, when Frankie Fact thinks about ice cream, he has these thoughts:

- Ice cream is cold.

- Ice cream comes in different colors.

- Ice cream comes in different flavors.

- Ice cream melts in the heat.

For You to Do

Notice that Frankie Fact didn't mention anything about how he feels about ice cream or which flavors he loves. It takes practice to notice the thoughts that come from your fact mind and to notice when Frankie Fact is speaking to you.

Let's practice identifying thoughts that Frankie Fact would like. Read the following story and underline as many fact-mind thoughts as you can.

It's back-to-school time, and Sheila needs new shoes. She has picked out a pair that she really, really wants. They cost $150. When she talks to her parents about getting them, her mom says no. Her dad tells her the shoes are too expensive and they have to buy other things Sheila needs for going back to school. They have only $50 to spend on shoes. Sheila does have some money in her savings, but it is not enough; she has only $25. Sheila's mom has found another pair of shoes that costs $50 and fits within the budget, but Sheila does not like them. Sheila is mad about this and finds herself arguing with her parents every day about getting the shoes she wants and not the ones her parents can afford. Her parents tell her that if she wants to do some work in her father's shop to earn the extra money, she can. Sheila doesn't like this idea because the work in her father's shop is boring and no fun. She wants to be able to get the shoes she likes without having to do any extra work. Sheila is so angry that she yells and cries when talking about it to her parents.

People Have Different Feelings

For You to Know

Two people can have completely different feelings about the exact same situation.

In activity 2, we got to know Frankie Fact. Now let's get to know his cousin, Fiona Feeling. Remember that Frankie and Fiona work together in your mind, and when they get along they help you make good decisions. When they don't get along, it can cause problems.

Like Frankie, Fiona Feeling has some favorite ways of thinking. She focuses on how she feels about a situation and her opinions on a subject. Fiona Feeling thinks most about what *she* wants to do or say, and she usually wants to do or say them right away. Sometimes Fiona struggles to understand why others have a different opinion about something. For example, when Fiona Feeling thinks about ice cream, these are her thoughts:

- Ice cream is my favorite.

- I love chocolate ice cream.

- Chocolate ice cream is the best.

- I want chocolate ice cream right now!

For You to Do

Notice that Fiona Feeling did not mention any facts about ice cream. It takes practice to notice when Fiona Feeling is speaking to you. Let's practice identifying thoughts that Fiona Feeling would like. Go back to Sheila's story in activity 2 and circle as many feeling-mind thoughts as you can.

Creating a Full Mind

For You to Know

Mindfulness means paying attention on purpose to what is important. When you are practicing mindfulness, you want to be sure that your mind is full of both facts and feelings. When you have the right balance of facts and feelings in your mind, it is easier to take control of your actions and manage your feelings.

A first step in taking control of your mind is to learn how to be mindful. With practice, you can learn how to notice when your feelings are filling up your mind too quickly, and you can slow your feelings down by adding in some facts. A main goal when practicing mindfulness is to find your own balance of noticing the facts about the world around you and noticing the feelings you have about those facts.

In this activity, let's pretend that your mind is a jar, the facts are rocks, and your feelings are sand. You are going to practice filling your mind so it is full with both facts and feelings. It will be important for you to remember these things as you practice:

- If your mind fills up with feelings first, there won't be room for any facts.

- Facts are the "who, what, when, and where" of what you notice when you see or hear something.

- Feelings come from how you feel about those facts.

- It is normal for two different people to have different feelings about the same facts.

- It is important to remember that there is no right way to feel about facts. You just want to be sure to notice both the facts and your feelings.

For You to Do

For this activity, you'll need a jar, some rocks, a container of sand, and a cup of water. To be mindful, it is important for you to notice the facts (the rocks) and to be sure they are put in your mind (the jar) before your feelings (the sand) take over. If your feelings fill up your mind first, you will not have room for all the facts!

1. Pick a situation and write down the facts (who, what, when, where) here:

   _____

   _____

   _____

2. Now pick out what feelings you have based on those facts. Write your feelings here:

   _____

   _____

3. Fill up your jar with just facts and make sure that your facts fit all the way in your jar. Do you see all the empty spaces between your rocks? That is where your feelings will fit!

4. Empty your jar, and save all the rocks that fit in close by. Now quickly fill up your jar with sand. Then try to put your rocks back in. Do they fit? They usually won't fit the same way if your jar is already filled with sand.

5. Now start again. Have your rocks ready and your sand back in your container. This time, practice putting in some rocks first, while stating what the facts are. Then pour your sand in to fill in the space around the rocks while stating what your feelings are. You might need to shake your jar gently so that the sand fills in the space around your rocks.

6. If there is any space left in your jar after filling it with rocks and sand, fill those spaces with water. Water represents help: the people you can go to for support, answers, and advice. If you don't see any room in your jar, try slowly adding a little water anyway. Did you notice you could add some water even when it didn't look like there was room? That is a reminder that we can always find room for a little advice or support, even if we don't think we need it.

Congratulations! You are on your way to being mindful, and you are learning how to notice both facts and feelings.

More for You to Do

The more that you practice noticing both the facts and your feelings, the better you will be at balancing the two. With balance, your actions will become more helpful and you will feel more in control.

Think about a problem you are having. In the jar below, write down the facts of the situation and your feelings about the facts. Try to fit both facts (the rocks) and feelings (the sand) in your mind (the jar).

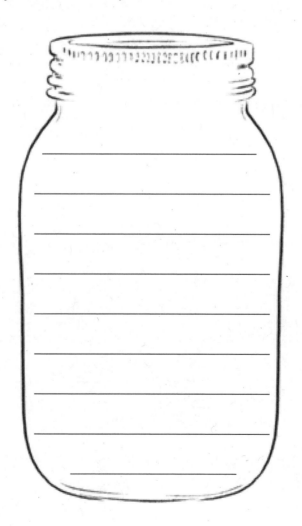

Was it easy or hard to fit all these facts and feelings in? What advice might someone else have to add? You can make a guess, or you can ask someone. Remember that advice or support from others is like adding some water into your jar of rocks and sand. No matter how full your jar is with rocks and sand, there will always be room for a little water (advice).

For You to Know

Things that hurt you in the past and worries about the future often get in the way of noticing what is happening in the present moment. If you can focus your mind on just what is happening right now, you can give yourself a break from feelings of sadness, hurt, or anger about the past and of fear or nervousness about what might happen in the future.

It can be helpful to think of the present moment, the moment you are in right now, as a gift. When you notice a strong feeling, try to ask yourself if the feeling is about something that is happening right now or if it is about something that hasn't happened yet. If your feeling isn't about something going on right now in the present moment, use the acronym GIFT to focus your mind back to the here and now. An acronym is a reminder word formed from the beginning letters of an idea. Think of the acronym GIFT as a present you are giving to yourself.

G—Get

I—into

F—focusing on

T—the present moment

For You to Do

Draw a picture below of the gift you will be giving yourself. Think of what is happening right now, and write the facts about right now inside your gift. Outside, draw your hurts from the past or your worries about the future.

For You to Know

It takes a lot of practice to find your balance of facts and feelings. You can never practice mindfulness too much. Just like riding a bike, the more you practice mindfulness, the easier it becomes to find your balance.

Now that you have learned a little about what mindfulness is, let's talk about different ways you can practice being mindful. You can practice being mindful for bits of time every day. You don't need to have this workbook with you to practice.

Here are some ways you can practice being mindful:

- Pay attention to your breathing. While doing this for a few minutes, notice if a thought, feeling, or sound catches your attention and say to yourself, *That is a thought* (or feeling or sound), then turn your focus back to just breathing. This is an important activity you can practice many times every day.

- Review activity 4. What facts can you see around you? Those are your rocks in the jar. How do you feel about the facts? Your feelings about the facts become the sand filling up the space around the rocks in your jar. The jar is your mind, full of facts and feelings.

- Think about what you need to do and what you want to do. Let's say that after school you need to get your homework done but you want to watch a movie. Is there a way to do your homework and still watch some of the movie? This can be tricky to practice, but just because something is tricky doesn't mean it's not possible. Find a way to balance what you need to do and what you want to do.

- If you notice a thought or a feeling getting in the way of doing what you need to do, try to focus on just doing one thing at a time. It is best to focus on what you need to do first (for example, focus on a chore) and just pay attention to what is needed to get that chore done. You may surprise yourself by getting "needs" done faster when you are not distracted by your thoughts, feelings, or "wants."

For You to Do

Make a list of things you need to do. List thoughts and feelings you have about doing each. Then, list mindfulness practices you could use to get your need finished so you have time for what you want. It might be helpful to write down what you want and think of it as a prize for doing what is needed.

What You Need to Do Right Now	Thoughts	Feelings	Mindfulness Skills to Use	Wants (Your Reward)
Homework	Homework is boring. I want to watch a movie. It feels good to be done and not worry about my homework.	Frustrated Angry Distracted	GIFT (Get into focusing on the present moment.) Notice and listen to your helpful thoughts.	I get to watch my favorite movie.

What You Need to Do Right Now	Thoughts	Feelings	Mindfulness Skills to Use	Wants (Your Reward)

Don't Let Your Emotions Run Your Life for Kids

Section 2

Understanding Your Feelings

Very strong feelings that can seem out of control can be called your "big" feelings, and less intense feelings can be called your "small" feelings. This section of your workbook includes activities that will help you understand more about both kinds of feelings. At http://www .newharbinger.com/38594, you can also download a bonus activity called "Identifying Your Target Feelings."

Feelings can be uncomfortable, and sometimes you may want to pretend uncomfortable feelings aren't there. While that is a normal response, it is important to know that your uncomfortable feelings will actually go away much faster when you notice them and figure out why they popped up in the first place. It is more helpful to know about and label a feeling when you have it than to ignore a feeling or pretend it isn't there. When you notice and label your feelings, it helps your brain understand that what you feel is normal.

Remember, *all* your feelings are important, even the uncomfortable ones. When you notice an excited feeling, it is usually a signal that you might really enjoy something. But when you notice an uncomfortable feeling, it is usually a signal that you might dislike something. When you notice this signal, or feeling, on purpose, your brain starts to understand why it is there and helps you figure out what to say or do to make the feeling stay small or go away. Noticing and understanding your feelings is a big first step in helping you gain control of both your feelings and your behaviors.

For You to Know

In the caveman days, anger would have helped you survive by sending your body signals and lots of energy to help you fight off large, scary animals. This could have saved your life and the life of your family. Today, anger can still send your body those strong signals, even if you are not in a life-or-death situation. Noticing the anger signals you feel in your body can help you feel more in control.

Anger is a feeling that is meant to help you protect yourself and those you care about. Anger can also help you define goals. When someone or something tries to block your goal, you might get angry. If you are trying to study for a test and you hear your brother being loud in the background, you might get angry because his loud sounds are getting in the way of your goal of studying. Anger can give you the energy to do helpful behaviors, like asking your brother to be quiet while you are studying. Anger can also lead to unhelpful behaviors when it feels out of control, such as yelling, hitting, and throwing things.

When you recognize that you are feeling anger and notice where that anger is coming from, you will have more control to use your anger in a helpful way by setting a limit or asking for what you want or need. Anger can be big or small. It is usually easier to act on anger in helpful ways when we notice the small forms of anger.

Don't Let Your Emotions Run Your Life for Kids

For You to Do

Look through these anger words and circle the experiences you've noticed in yourself:

Rage   Frustrated

Annoyed   Grouchy

Mad   Grumpy

Irritated

Add any other anger words that you have for your experience: _____

_____

What Causes Anger?

Anger is a normal response to having a goal blocked. Listed below are things that often start anger:

- You don't get what you want or need.

- Someone takes your things without asking.

- You think someone or something is unfair.

If you think of other things not listed that have started anger for you, use these blank lines to write them down:

_____

_____

How You React to Anger

When you are feeling angry, you will usually notice one or more of the following signals. Circle the experiences you've noticed in yourself.

Fast heartbeat

Wanting to hit someone or explode

Hot face

Wanting to hurt someone

Clenched fists

Crying

Scrunched face and eyes

Pounding, throwing things, breaking things

If a signal you've noticed isn't listed, you can use the blank lines to add it:

_____

_____

More for You to Do

In the space below, write about or draw how anger looks and feels to you.

> ## *For You to Know*
>
> Feeling anxiety is a normal part of life. It can be very important, but it does not always help us reach our goals.

Anxiety sometimes tells us that we are in danger. If you are about to jump from a really high place, you probably feel anxiety. This is your brain's way of telling you that this might not be a good idea and that you could get hurt. In situations like this, it is important to listen to your anxiety; it is helping you keep safe. Feeling butterflies in your stomach when taking a test is a sign of anxiety that actually helps you focus and do your best.

Anxiety is not always helpful. Sometimes it can be so big that you freeze in your tracks when there is actually no danger. For example, if you feel anxiety right before your school concert and think you can't go on stage, you are going to miss out on having fun during your concert.

It is important to get to know what your anxiety feels like so you can learn to tell the difference between anxiety that is helping you and anxiety that is stopping you from being great or having fun.

For You to Do

Look through the anxiety words listed and circle the experiences you've noticed in yourself:

Nervous

Afraid

Uneasy

Worried

Panic

Overwhelmed

Frightened

Tense

Add any other anxiety words you have experienced for yourself: _____

_____

What Causes Anxiety?

Many different situations can cause anxiety:

- You don't know what is going to happen.

- You could be hurt or injured.

- You think you might fail or get in trouble.

- You think you might lose something important.

- You think you won't get the help you need.

- You are alone.

- You think you will be embarrassed.

If you think of other things that have started anxiety for you, use these blank lines to write them down:

_____

_____

How You React to Anxiety

Read the list below and circle the experiences you've noticed in yourself.

Fast heartbeat

Wanting to scream

Hot face

Hair standing on end

Lump in throat

Crying

Butterflies in stomach

Trouble breathing

Tight muscles

Feeling like you might throw up

If a signal you notice isn't listed, you can use the blank lines to add it: _____

_____

More for You to Do

In the space below, write about or draw how anxiety looks and feels to you.

> ### *For You to Know*
>
> *Envy* is the feeling you notice when someone else has something that you want or need. *Jealousy* is the feeling you notice when you don't want to lose someone or something that you already have. Both feelings can be helpful, but they can also get in your way.

Envy is helpful when it motivates you to work hard to achieve something you want or need for yourself. For example, when Karl wins the spelling bee, Josh might think, *Wow! I really want a spelling bee trophy. I should ask Karl how he studied to get helpful ideas.* But when envy feels out of control or too big, it can prompt you take something that you want or need from someone else. For example, if Josh's envy is out of control, he may try to steal Karl's trophy.

Jealousy can prompt you to do nice things to keep someone close to you who is already close to you. For example, if you are afraid your best friend is hanging out with the new kid at school more than with you, you might offer to play your best friend's favorite game at recess. This is a nice thing to do because it puts your friend's wishes first. But it is important to notice when jealous thoughts are making you want to control someone so that it feels, to you, like the person can't or won't leave you. For example, Kara noticed jealousy when her close friend Sam was spending more time with a new friend, Kelly, and less time with her. Kara started texting Sam over and over again when Sam was with Kelly, even after Sam asked Kara not to. Sam started spending less and less time with Kara because she felt controlled by Kara's constant texting. In this situation, jealousy got too big, prompting unhelpful action (texting over and over) that got in the way of Kara's friendship with Sam.

For You to Do

Look through the envy and jealousy words listed below, and circle the ones you've experienced in yourself:

Shy

Wanting something

Greedy

Resentful

Payback

Doubtful

Hate

Uncertainty

Fear of losing something you have

Add any other envy or jealousy words you have experienced: _____

_____

What Causes Envy or Jealousy?

Envy or jealousy can arise for many reasons:

- You want or need something you don't have.

- You don't want to lose something you already have.

- You think someone has what you want or need.

- You think someone will take what is already yours.

- You feel rejected or disliked by others.

- You feel lonely.

- You think you are not being treated the same as others.

If you think of things not listed that have started envy or jealousy for you, use these blank lines to write them down: _____

_____

How You React to Envy or Jealousy

Read the list below and circle the things you've experienced in yourself.

Wanting to take things from others

Not wanting to share what you have

Hot face

Yelling

Lump in throat

Tantrums

Wanting to destroy what others have

Wanting to hurt others

Tight muscles

Demanding attention

Add any other envy or jealousy signals you may have noticed: _____

_____

More for You to Do

Use one of the boxes below to write about or draw how envy looks and feels to you. Use the other box to show how jealousy looks and feels to you.

Guilt and Shame

For You to Know

Guilt and shame are two different feelings that often come together. Guilt is a signal that you did something against your own values, and it can be helpful. Shame is a signal that often makes you think bad things about yourself. You feel it when you have gone against the values of other people, and they don't like you because of that.

Guilt is the feeling you have when you know that you've broken a rule. This feeling is telling you to make a better choice next time or to try to remember the rule so you don't break it again. Allow yourself to feel guilt for a little while. It will help you remember to make a better choice next time.

Shame is different from guilt. It can happen when guilt is too big and turns into feeling bad about yourself or disliking yourself. For example, if you break a rule on accident, maybe because you forgot, and then start to think that you are stupid because you forgot and that others won't like you anymore, you are feeling shame. Remember that all people are good inside, and do not let the shame stick around. Letting the feeling of shame stick around will make you feel bad about yourself as a person, and that will not be helpful.

For You to Do

Look through these guilt and shame words, and circle those you've experienced yourself:

Rejection

Humiliated

Embarrassed

Taking blame

Uncomfortable

Frightened

Tense

Regret

Sorry

Add any other guilt or shame words you have experienced: _____

_____

What Causes Guilt or Shame?

Here are some possible causes of guilt or shame:

- Thinking you did something wrong

- Doing something against your values

- Getting in trouble

- Fighting with friends or family

- Finding out you hurt someone

- Being told you are bad

- Feeling embarrassed

Add any others you think of: _____

_____

How You React to Guilt or Shame

Circle the items on the list below that you have experienced yourself.

Wanting to disappear

Hiding from others

No eye contact with others

Shoulders hunched forward

Lump in throat

Crying

Sick to stomach

Looking down

Feeling like a bad person

Feeling like you might throw up

Add any others that are not listed: _____

_____

More for You to Do

Use one of the boxes below to write about or draw how guilt looks and feels to
you. Use the other box to show how shame looks and feels to you.

Feeling Overwhelmed and Excited

> ## *For You to Know*
>
> People are excited by different things. Some things that you might find exciting and fun might be overwhelming and scary to others.

When you have a big project to do and are not sure where to start, you might be overwhelmed. Being overwhelmed can be an uncomfortable feeling, and when you are overwhelmed it is hard for you to do your best. It can be difficult to pick just one thing to start with.

Being excited can be fun and feel good. When you are about to do something really fun, and you get a burst of energy in your body, you are excited. Can you think of a time when you were so excited that you couldn't stand it? Have you ever been so excited that it felt like you couldn't control your body? Excitement can be a fun feeling, but it can also be overwhelming.

For You to Do

Look through these overwhelmed and excitement words, and circle the ones you've experienced yourself:

Wound up

Energized

Scattered

Jumpy

Emotional

Delighted

Restless

Distracted

Add any others you have experienced: _____

_____

What Causes Overwhelming or Exciting Feelings?

Situations like these can make you feel overwhelmed or excited:

- You think about something that you really want to do.

- You make new friends or meet new people.

- You think about something you have to do.

- You think about something big that already happened or that will happen in the future.

- There is a change in your daily routine.

- You want to share an idea or opinion with others.

- You think things are really, really good.

Add any others you think of: _____

_____

How You React to Being Overwhelmed or Excited

Circle the items in the list below that you have experienced yourself.

Fast heartbeat

Trouble sitting still

Difficulties focusing

Talking fast

Lots of energy

Having lots of thoughts

Being keyed up

Not listening to others

Wanting attention

Add any others not listed: _____

_____

More for You to Do

Use one of the boxes below to write about or draw how being overwhelmed looks
and feels to you. Use the other box to show how excitement looks and feels to you.

For You to Know

Love is a feeling of being close or connected to someone else. Sometimes you feel love because someone has done nice things for you. Sometimes you aren't sure why you feel love, and when this happens it can be confusing. Love helps us stay close with people we want to stay connected to, like family and special friends. Love can be a painful feeling if it doesn't fit the facts.

Love is the feeling you notice when someone you care about does things you like and helps either take care of you or brings you closer to a value or goal you have. This is when love fits the facts. When love fits the facts, it can feel good and can help you do nice things for someone else. For example, when his brother cleaned up their shared bedroom without asking Michael to help, Michael noticed feeling loved, because his brother had done work that benefited both of them without asking Michael for anything in return. Michael decided to do all their shared yard work the next day to show his appreciation for his brother. Michael noticed love that motivated him to helpful action.

Love can become unhelpful when you notice this feeling toward someone who does things to hurt you. Sometimes love can feel big, and you don't know if the person you feel love for is loving in return. When that happens, love can feel very confusing! For example, John noticed loving feelings toward Sarah, and he did nice things for her, like drawing pictures for her and inviting her to hang out at the park. Sarah laughed at John when he gave her pictures and asked her to go to the park. John felt confused because Sarah hurt him by laughing at him, and he started to realize she was not doing things to help him in return. This can happen and it can hurt, but it does not mean John did anything wrong. It just means that the love John feels for Sarah isn't helpful because she isn't helpful toward him and she isn't bringing him closer to any of his values or goals. John's love for Sarah doesn't fit the facts because he did nice things and she hurt him in return.

For You to Do

Look through the love words listed below, and circle the things you have experienced:

Like

Adore

Friendship

Affection

Add any others you have experienced that aren't listed: _____

_____

What Causes Love?

Love is a normal response to caring about someone you admire and who helps bring you closer to your values and goals. Listed below are common things that start love:

- Being with someone or something who makes you feel good about yourself

- Wanting to have someone or something with you at all times

- Wanting to help and take care of another person

If you think of other things that have started love for you, list them on the blank lines:

_____

_____

How You React to Love

Your body sends you signals that tell you about what you are feeling. When you are feeling love, you will usually notice the following signals in your body. Circle the things below that you have noticed in yourself.

Fast heartbeat

Excitement

Butterflies in stomach

Cheeks feeling warm or looking rosy

If a signal you've noticed isn't listed, you can add it on the blank lines:

_____

_____

More for You to Do

Write about or draw how love looks and feels to you.

For You to Know

Sadness tells you that you miss someone or something. It helps remind you that you care about people and things. Sadness can be uncomfortable and seem not so helpful when it gets really big, but it can help you know what your values are and that you care about people.

Just like every other emotion, sadness can be helpful even if it doesn't feel like it sometimes. You feel sadness when you have lost someone or something you care about, and you also feel sadness when things don't turn out the way you hoped they would. Sometimes it can be hard to know why you are feeling sad, but usually if you notice your sadness and think about it for a few minutes you will be able to tell where it is coming from. For example, one day Hank woke up feeling very sad. He didn't know why he was sad at first, and that really bothered him. When he sat and noticed his sadness on purpose, he was able to remember that a few days before he had tried really hard to make the soccer team and felt sad when he didn't make it. Then he remembered that today was the first soccer team practice. Hank noticed that his sadness didn't feel so big when he could understand where it was coming from.

When you recognize that you are feeling sad and you notice where it comes from, you will be better able to keep sadness from getting out of control. Sadness usually stays pretty small when you can notice what is causing it. Noticing sadness doesn't always make the sadness go away, but it can help!

For You to Do

Look through these sadness words, and circle the ones you have noticed in yourself:

Disappointment

Let down

Grieving

Depression

Unhappy

Gloomy

Rotten

Empty

Blue

Hopeless

Heartbroken

Add any others you have noticed in yourself:

_____

_____

What Causes Sadness?

Sadness is a normal response to missing someone or something. Listed below are common things that start sadness:

- Not being able to see someone or something you love

- Being alone

- Losing something you love

- Doing something wrong and disappointing others

- Having something not turn out the way you wanted

- Having plans change

If you think of other things that have started sadness for you, list them on the blank lines:

_____

_____

How You React to Sadness

Your body sends you signals that tell you about what you are feeling. When you are feeling sadness, you will usually notice the following signals in your body. Circle the experiences you have noticed in yourself.

Heavy stomach

Wanting to be alone

Crying

Being quiet

Hollow or empty chest

If a signal you've noticed isn't listed, you can add it on these blank lines:

_____

_____

More for You to Do

Write about or draw how sadness looks and feels to you.

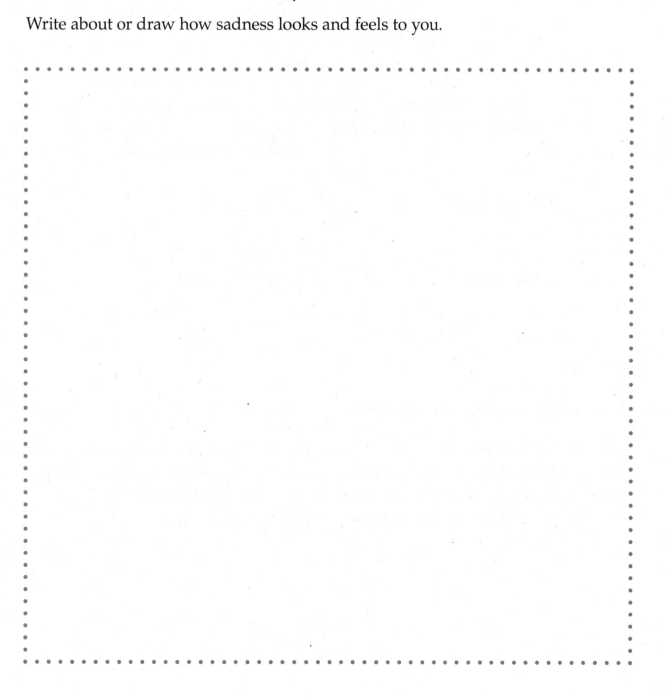

For You to Know

Most people usually like happiness and want more of this feeling. It is just as important to understand what makes you happy as it is to notice what makes you feel any other feeling. If you know what makes you happy, you can work on getting more of that in your life.

Happiness is a feeling you get when something turns out in a way you like. For example, Caleb noticed feeling happy when he woke up and his dad told him that there was too much snow to go to school. He liked that because he loves playing in the snow, and he started thinking of all the fun he could have outside.

Happiness can also come from being around people who are nice to you or from being with people who take care of you. For example, Laura noticed feeling happy while spending time with her relatives during a family get-together. Her aunt asked her about what she had been doing, and everyone listened to what she had to say. Laura likes it when people show interest in her. This made her very happy!

When you recognize that you are feeling happiness and you notice where it comes from, you will have more control because you will know what you can try to do to get your happiness back if it seems to be missing. Noticing happiness doesn't always make you instantly happy, but it can help!

For You to Do

Look through the happiness words listed below and circle the ones you have experienced in yourself:

Cheerful

Delight

Hopeful

Peaceful

Playful

Excited

Content

Pumped

Giggly

Add any others you have experienced for yourself: _____

_____

What Causes Happiness?

Happiness is a normal response to having something happen to you that you like. Listed below are common things that start this feeling:

- Getting something you want

- Spending time with someone you love

- Winning a game or award

- Having things go the way you wanted them to

If you think of other things that have started happiness for you, write them on the blank lines:

_____

_____

How You React to Happiness

Your body sends you signals that tell you about what you are feeling. When you are feeling happiness, you may notice the following signals in your body. Circle the experiences from the list below that you have noticed in yourself.

Fast heartbeat

Smiling

Laughing

Silliness

Increased energy

If a signal you've noticed isn't listed, you can add it on the blank lines:

_____

_____

More for You to Do

Write about or draw how happiness looks and feels to you.

Section 3

Working with Your Feelings

In section 2, you read about some of the common feelings people have. In this section, you will learn about how feelings come in different sizes, depending on the situation you are in, and about how you can manage or change your feelings. As you work on learning more about feelings in this section, it will help to look back to what you learned about feelings in section 2.

Thoughts or Feelings?

For You to Know

Thoughts and feelings can be confusing, and they are not the same thing. Learning the difference can help you know what to do in each situation.

You are going to learn a lot about thoughts and feelings in this book. It is important for you to know the difference, because changing the way you think about something can actually change the way you feel. Let's review some of the differences between the two.

Thoughts

Thoughts are like sentences in your mind; for example, the statement "I feel like you're not listening to me" is actually a thought: *I think you are not listening to me.*

Just having a thought can change your feelings. For example, thinking about something sad can actually make you feel sad. This also works in reverse. If you are sad and think about something happy, your feeling of sadness can change.

Thoughts are not always true. You can think to yourself that the sky is green, but when you look out the window you see that your thought doesn't fit the facts. This can happen a lot, and it's important to learn to check whether your thoughts fit the facts.

Don't Let Your Emotions Run Your Life for Kids

Feelings

Feelings are shorter than thoughts and usually take only around three words to express; for example, "I feel angry" expresses a feeling, while "I think you are not listening to me" is a thought. Notice that "I think you are not listening to me" is not a fact because we don't know for sure that someone is not listening. This is why it is important to notice the difference between thoughts and feelings. You can always check in with the person to see if your thoughts are true.

Your feelings are your brain's way of telling you important things about what is going on. You will learn more about this in activity 16.

Feelings can be very overwhelming and intense. In fact, feelings can be so intense that they can make it hard for you to know if your thoughts fit the facts.

For You to Do

Learning to tell the difference between thoughts and feelings takes practice. Use this chart to practice recording the different thoughts and feelings you have. At http://www.newharbinger.com/38594, you can download a copy so that you can use it over and over. Also, take this opportunity to see if your thought fits the facts. Ask yourself, *Are my thoughts telling me the truth?* Remember that practice makes perfect!

Situation	*Thought*	*What Are the Facts?*	*Feeling*
I'm trying to tell Mom about my day, but she's looking at her phone.	*Mom isn't listening.*	*Mom is looking at her phone. I don't know for sure if she's listening.* (Hint: You can check with your mom by asking, "Are you listening?"	*Frustrated*

Why Do You Have Feelings?

Gathering information from your feelings is like putting together all the pieces of a pie.

P—Feelings help **protect** you or tell you that you need to change your behavior. When you have a strong feeling, it is your brain's way of telling you that you need to change your behavior or act quickly. For example, if someone hurts you, you might feel sad or angry. These feelings can prompt you to tell an adult that you need some help.

I—Feelings give you **information** about your environment, and they can give others information about you. If you are in danger, you get scared. The feeling of fear tells you that you need to look around and make sure you are safe. When you are sad, you might show your sadness by crying. This tells those around you that you need comforting. If you do not show your feelings or talk about them, others will not know you need help.

E—Emotions are **not equal** to facts! Big feelings, or emotions, can be strong and feel like they are facts about the world. For example, you might have fear before meeting a new teacher or friend, but that does not mean you are actually in danger. If your friend breaks your favorite toy, it would make sense that you might be angry. Your feeling mind might tell you to break his toy in return, but if you listen to your fact mind urging you to talk to your friend, you might learn it was an accident.

For You to Do

When you have a strong feeling, it can be hard to remember all this information about feelings. It can be especially hard when you are uncomfortable with your feeling and you just want it to go away! Let's make a PIE to help us remember this important information about feelings.

What you need:

- Paper plate

- Construction paper (and any other art supplies you would like)

- Markers, crayons, or pencils

- Scissors

- Stapler

Steps:

1. The plate is going to be like a pie tin. Draw four pieces on your plate.

2. Using a marker, crayon, or pencil, label the four sections P, I, E, and ? Write in the information about each letter on the sections of your pie tin. For example, on the P section, you could write "protection" or "change." On the I section, you could write "information for me and others." On the E section, you could write "not equal to facts." And on the ? section, you could write "Why do we have feelings?"

3. Now you are ready to create the pie that will cover your plate. Trace the circle of your pie tin on the construction paper.

4. Cut your pie into four parts and label them with P-I-E-?

5. Match the letters on your pie with the letters on your tin, and staple around the edge. You might want adult help with this step.

You can flip back each piece of pie and quiz yourself on the reasons we have emotions. Practice using this tool when learning about feelings.

Does Your Feeling Fit the Facts?

For You to Know

Sometimes your feelings don't fit the facts and they get in your way. When your feelings do fit the facts, they can tell you about your values, your goals, and what is important to you. You *can* figure out whether your feelings fit the facts.

If your feeling is helping you reach a goal, it likely fits the facts. If your feeling is getting in your way, it could be that it doesn't fit the facts. Keep these basic instructions in mind when you're trying to figure out if your feeling fits the facts:

1. Identify and label your feeling. Doing this helps your brain understand why you feel the way you do.

   Example: You notice tears and a heavy feeling in your stomach, and this helps you identify that you are feeling sad. You would notice and label your feeling as "sadness."

2. Identify what happened right before you first noticed your feeling.

   Example: Your brother borrowed your favorite shirt and accidentally got a stain on it. You noticed the stain right before you noticed the heavy feeling in your stomach, and right after noticing that heavy feeling your eyes filled with tears.

Don't Let Your Emotions Run Your Life for Kids

3. Notice if you are thinking about a worst-case scenario. When this happens, it can feel like the worst-case scenario is actually happening. Ask yourself whether it is happening or not.

   Example: You notice the thought *That stain will never come out of my favorite shirt, and now it's ruined forever.* Remember, it is possible that the worst-case scenario *could* happen, but right now it is important to know that you haven't tried to wash the stain out and you don't know that it won't come out. The worst-case scenario is not happening.

4. Identify a possible goal that is coming from your feeling.

   Example: You saved up your allowance for three whole weeks to buy this shirt, and it's your favorite of all your shirts. You know it would take at least three more weeks to replace it. Your sadness could be telling you that it's hard to lose something you worked hard to earn. This might prompt you to ask your brother to repay you somehow. You might ask if he would try to get the stain out, or if he would agree to replace your shirt with his own money if the stain doesn't come out.

For You to Do

Now practice this on your own. Ask yourself:

What is my big feeling? This could be one of your target feelings. Write it down here:

_____

Was there an event that started this feeling? Write down whatever you noticed happening right before your feeling started:

_____

_____

Are you imagining a worst-case scenario? Has that actually happened? Remember, if it hasn't happened, it might not fit the facts. Write about your worst-case scenario and whether it fits the facts:

_____

_____

_____

Keep in mind that there is a reason for your feeling; it might be telling you something. Can you think of a goal your feeling is helping you get to? Does your feeling fit the facts? What is your feeling trying to tell you? List your ideas here:

_____

_____

_____

More for You to Do

Using this chart, make a list of ways your feelings help you. For example, being mad at someone might help you tell that person that she is not treating you very well, and being afraid might help you run away from danger. Make another list of feelings that get in your way. Remember, it is normal for you to have feelings that sometimes help you and sometimes get in your way.

How Feelings Help You	*How Feelings Get in Your Way*
Fear helps me identify danger and get away from it quickly. That can keep me safe.	*It's hard not to yell when I'm angry. When I yell, I get in trouble and the person I'm yelling at might hear only my loud voice but not the words I'm saying.*

Feelings Are Constantly Changing

> ## *For You to Know*
>
> Feelings can be confusing. They can change from one minute to the next, and you can even have more than one feeling at a time!

People can have more than one feeling at a time, and feelings can come one right after another like cars on a busy highway. The feeling you have first is called the primary feeling. It appears quickly, and it can impact your urges and actions in negative ways. The feelings that come next are called the secondary feelings. They hang around a little longer.

Let's read an example of primary and secondary feelings in action.

You've been invited to a friend's house for a sleepover. You are *so* anxious! That's your primary feeling. In fact, your anxiety is so big that you don't go to the sleepover. This makes your friend sad because she wanted to see you. Now you feel sad and guilty because your not being at the sleepover hurt your friend's feelings. Sadness and guilt are your secondary feelings.

Don't Let Your Emotions Run Your Life for Kids

For You to Do

Learning to identify your primary and secondary feelings takes practice. For a week keep a log of situations and primary and secondary feelings that you experience. You can download a copy of this log at http://www.newharbinger .com/38594.

Day	Situation	Primary Feeling (Happens first, happens fast!)	Secondary Feeling (Happens second, hangs around!)
Monday			
Tuesday			
Wednesday			
Thursday			
Friday			
Saturday			
Sunday			

Things to think about: What did you notice? Was there a primary feeling that happened more often? Was there a secondary feeling that you felt more often than others?

Dear Feeling...

For You to Know

Feelings are only a part of who you are. With practice, you can learn to control them.

When you have intense feelings, it can feel as if they take over and you have no choice but to physically act out. The truth is, you can have an intense feeling and not let that feeling take control of your physical actions. When you take the time to observe and describe your feeling, you can think about what actions will be more helpful. This gives you more control because you can choose what actions to do. Let's look at one example of what can happen when an intense feeling takes control.

Kyle is having a rough day; he overslept and then was late to school. At lunchtime, Kyle is carrying his tray through the crowded lunchroom. Jason is also walking through the lunchroom and is not watching where he is going. Jason runs into Kyle, knocking his lunch to the ground. Kyle is angry! He turns to Jason, punches him, and a fight begins.

Teachers rush over and break up the fight. Kyle is in trouble now and has to go to the principal's office. This seems to be happening to him a lot lately. Kyle gets so angry that he feels out of control, as if he cannot control his actions.

For You to Do

Place an empty chair across from you. Imagine that sitting in the chair is the thing that makes Kyle want to hit Jason, that makes him feel as if he is going to explode. Sitting in the chair is the thing that makes Kyle feel out of control!

What do you think is sitting in the chair? For Kyle, ANGER is sitting in the chair. Anger is taking control of Kyle's actions, and he needs to work on becoming stronger than his anger. Help Kyle write a letter to Anger.

Dear Anger,

_____

_____

_____

_____

_____

_____

_____

_____

Sincerely,

Kyle

More for You to Do

Now choose a feeling you struggle with, and write a letter to that feeling. Writing a letter to your feeling will help you observe and describe your feeling and the behaviors you have when you experience that feeling.

Dear _____,

_____

_____

_____

_____

_____

_____

_____

_____

Sincerely,

_____

You Don't Have to Act on Your Urge
Activity 20

> ## *For You to Know*
>
> By being aware of your thoughts and feelings (which is part of mindfulness) you can learn to notice urges and control your actions.

In activity 19, Kyle was so angry that he hit Jason, and a fight broke out in the cafeteria. Kyle got in trouble because of the fight, not because he was angry.

Let's slow it down…

Feeling: Kyle is feeling angry.

Urge: Kyle has the urge to hit Jason.

Action: Kyle acts on the urge and hits Jason.

Situations like these happen fast, and your feelings and urges can be overwhelming! Learning to identify your urges and possible reactions to them can help.

Let's look at the example of Kyle again. Here are some possible urges he may have in reaction to anger:

- Hit

- Scream

- Walk away

- Throw something

- Talk it out

When choosing how to respond to your emotion, it is important to think about your choices. Which choice will lead to you feeling good about yourself and which choice will help you not get in trouble, as Kyle did in our example.

You will likely find it easier to identify your feeling, urge, and action in less emotional situations first. Practice as much as possible, so that in a really big moment you can make a good choice about whether or not to act on your urge.

For You to Do

Practice identifying your feeling, urge, and action. Record the results in the chart below, or download a copy at http://www.newharbinger.com/38594. There is also a column for you to list the helpful action you chose.

	Event	*Feeling*	*Urge*	*Action You Chose*
Practice #1				
Practice #2				
Practice #3				
Practice #4				

Notice whether there were times when you realized that you did not have to act on your urge. Practice often! The more times you practice, the easier it will become for you to make better decisions in the moment.

Activity 21

Situation, Feeling, Intensity Game

For You to Know

Different people have different feelings when in the same situation. This is totally normal. People have different intensities of feelings as well; this is also normal.

Having different feelings and different intensities of feelings is not good or bad, right or wrong; it's just different. The activity that follows is a game you can play as often as you like to help you practice identifying what feelings you have and how intense, or strong, they are. You can play with friends, siblings, or even your parents. Parents need to practice these skills too!

When you play, talk with the other players about why they choose the feeling and intensity they do.

Don't Let Your Emotions Run Your Life for Kids

For You to Do

Photocopy the cards on the next few pages and cut them out (or download copies of them from http://www.newharbinger.com/38594). There are blank situation cards you can add to and a blank feeling card for you to add any feeling that may not be listed. There are two variations to using these cards as a game, and at the website for this book you can download an additional set of cards for a third variation.

Be creative and have some fun! The goal is to practice identifying feelings and the intensity you would feel. As you move through the exercises in this book, you can come back to this game and talk about what tool you might use to change the intensity.

Variation 1

1. Make enough copies of the feeling and intensity cards so that each player has a full set. Make one copy of the situation cards.

2. Cut out the three sets of cards.

3. Each person playing gets one of each feeling card and one of each intensity card (1–10).

4. Place the situation cards facedown in the middle of the table.

5. The player whose turn it is picks a card and lays it faceup.

6. The other players each decide which feeling makes sense to them and lays down that card in front of them, along with the intensity they would feel.

7. Discuss any differences or similarities among the players. Remember that everyone might have a different feeling and intensity.

8. The game continues until all situation cards have been turned over and discussed.

Variation 2

1. Make a copy of the intensity cards for each person who will be playing.

2. Cut out the situation, feeling, and intensity cards.

3. Find a large space where you can move around and run.

4. Tape feelings cards on a far wall, with a little space between each one.

5. Players each hold their own intensity cards (1–10).

6. Put all the situation cards in a basket.

7. In turn, draw a situation card out of the basket, read it, decide which feeling you would have, then run as fast as you can to the feeling.

8. Hold up the intensity card when you get there.

9. Discuss with other players the feeling you chose and the intensity you felt.

10. The game is over when all situations have been discussed.

Feeling Cards

Anger	Fear	Jealousy
Guilt	Overwhelmed or Excited	Love
Sadness	Happiness	_____

Intensity Cards

1	2	3
4	5	6
7	8	9
10		

Situation Cards

Your brother takes your favorite toy.	Someone at school takes your place in line.	Your sister calls you a name.
The family plans change! You can't go to the zoo (or your favorite place).	Your classmate is sitting very close to you.	You lose your favorite toy or special item.
You lose a game.	You blame your brother for something, and he gets in trouble	You want to tell your mom a story, but she is listening to your sister.
You get exactly what you wanted for your birthday.	Your sister gets your favorite thing for *her* birthday.	A friend at school teases you.
You are meeting your new teacher for the first time.	You have to give a presentation in front of the class.	You have to take a test.
You are at a birthday party, and everyone is having the best time ever!	You and your brother are running around playing your favorite game. It is *such* a burst of energy!	You are left out of a game at school.

Your Piggy Bank of Happy Moments

For You to Know

It can be hard to notice things that make you feel good when your really big feelings are about the things that make you feel uncomfortable. Noticing what makes you feel good can change the way you feel because it can take your thoughts away from whatever is making you not feel so good.

When a big feeling pops up, it can be hard to imagine that it will ever go away. Sometimes big feelings that do not feel so good get in the way of remembering activities that can help you feel better. It can help to create a "piggy bank" that holds "happy moments."

Instead of coins, you can list activities that you like to do on strips of paper. Your bank could be a jar that holds your strips of paper, just like a piggy bank holds coins. Whenever you notice that you don't feel happy, you can go to your bank and try some things you have listed to see if they help you feel better.

Don't Let Your Emotions Run Your Life for Kids

For You to Do

What things make you feel good inside? Do you know? Check off things on this list if you think they could make you feel good. (You can add something you like if it's not on the list.)

☐ Riding my bike   ☐ Working with tools

☐ Watching a movie   ☐ Drawing

☐ Watching television   ☐ Playing a sport

☐ Talking to a friend   ☐ Playing video games

☐ Spending time with family   ☐ Listening to music

☐ Going on a trip   ☐ Other: _____

☐ Baking   ☐ Other: _____

☐ Playing a board game   ☐ Other: _____

Now that you have some ideas, let's play a game. Imagine that the ideas checked off on your list are like coins. Every time you do something you like on the list, you get to add a coin to your piggy bank. At times when you don't feel so good, take a coin out of your piggy bank. Having a lot of times when you don't feel good probably means that your piggy bank is pretty close to empty. Your goal is to always keep a few coins in the piggy bank. An empty piggy bank just means it is time for you to focus on some more feel-good moments.

More for You to Do

Draw a piggy bank in the space below. Think of some things you have done in the past week that made you feel good, and list those in your piggy bank. Does your bank look full? Have you done many feel-good things this past week? If not, brainstorm some ideas of things you can do this week to feel good, and write them down in your piggy bank.

Visit http://www.newharbinger.com/38594 for a bonus activity called "Soothing Yourself with Happy Moments."

Don't Let Your Emotions Run Your Life for Kids

Section 4

Creating Your Skills Toolbox

So far in this workbook you have learned about your different feelings and different things that start and influence these feelings. Now, you are going to figure out what to do to manage your feelings. You will need some coping skills, or tools. Your tools may be different from the tools another person might use, and that is okay. Just as a gardener or plumber needs different tools, you will need different coping skills, or different tools, to fix your feelings than other people might need to fix theirs.

This section is filled with ideas for ways to cope with your feelings. As you learn and practice these ideas, you might want to think of them as tools for your personal "skills toolbox," and it will be helpful to create your own reminders of what tools you like the most and why you like them.

What does this toolbox have to look like? It can look any way that you want. You can make note cards of your favorite skills so that you can practice them wherever you go. And guess what? That stack of note cards can be your toolbox!

There is no right or wrong way to start your skills toolbox. The point is just to make reminders of the tools you learn in this workbook as you learn them so that you can take them with you wherever you go.

At http://www.newharbinger.com/38594, section 7 includes four bonus activities you can download to help you make the most of your toolbox: "What Tools Do You Use for the Job?" "When Your Tools Are Not Working," "Practicing with the Tools You Have," and "It's a RAP."

Be creative and have fun!

Activity 23 Planting SEEDS in Your Skills Garden

For You to Know

If your body is tired or rundown, it will be very hard to gain control of your feelings. This is why it is important for you to "plant a garden" of basic skills, or tools, so that your body is not adding extra feelings and extra stress to your day.

SEEDS is an acronym to help you remember the importance of sleep, eating healthy, exercise, downtime, and socializing. You need to plant SEEDS before you can expect your skills garden to grow. Just like a real garden, planting seeds and growing a garden takes time. Here is a list of basic seeds to plant in your garden:

S—Sleep helps your brain and your body reset after each day. It is important to get the right amount of sleep each night. From nine to eleven hours of sleep is recommended for school-age children. How much sleep do you get? Do you feel better when you go to bed and wake up at the same time every day? Do you have trouble falling asleep or staying asleep, or do you wake up earlier than you want to in the morning? If so, you can try a sleep meditation.

E—Eating healthy foods helps your brain and body have energy that can help you better control your emotions. Are there healthy foods you could try to eat more often and foods you could try to eat less of? This does not mean you can never have a treat. Just make sure you are also eating healthy!

E—General guidelines state that children between ages six and twelve should get one hour or more of **exercise** most days. They also suggest that kids this age get about fifteen minutes or more of exercise in chunks every day, with no more than two hours going by without any exercise. Even small amounts of exercise can help your brain think more clearly and can distract you from your feelings for a while.

Don't Let Your Emotions Run Your Life for Kids

What activities or exercises do you already do? Are there others you can try on the days you might not be very active?

D—Downtime is important. It is a chance to give yourself a break. Even if it is just five minutes of not watching TV, talking to anyone, or doing homework, having downtime helps you notice your feelings so that you can figure out what to do to respond to them.

S—Socializing with others is also important, though sometimes it can be hard to find the right balance. Do you spend much time with others? Do you wish you had more time to yourself? Thinking about the social activities you wish you could do more of and the ones you wish you did not have to do so much can help you develop a plan for getting a balance of social activities in your day.

Visit http://www.newharbinger.com/38594 for a bonus activity called "Am I at Risk for Big Feelings Right Now?"

For You to Do

List your SEEDS plan here:

Sleep: _____

_____

Eating healthy: _____

_____

Exercise: _____

_____

Downtime: _____

_____

Socializing: _____

_____

More for You to Do

What SEEDS did you plant? Draw a picture of yourself standing in your garden.

How do you think you will feel when your garden starts to grow? How long do you think it will take your SEEDS to grow into plants? Write a sentence or two to describe this.

_____

_____

_____

Tools to Help You Shrink Your Feelings

For You to Know

The first tools you want in your toolbox are ones that can help you shrink your feeling so you can then fix a problem.

You will often notice a feeling when there is some problem in your life. Earlier in this workbook, you learned that your feelings are usually telling you something; for example, "Hey! Let's fix this problem!" The hard part is, sometimes your feeling is so big that you feel like you cannot make good decisions. When this happens, you might accidentally make a problem worse instead of fixing it.

You might not realize this, but you probably already have some tools you can use to fix this. Before you learn brand-new tools, let's figure out what tools you already have to help shrink a feeling. It might take some work to figure out how your tools currently help you, and how you can use them differently. Let's read about Jenny as an example.

Jenny often struggles with a big feeling of anger. Her anger used to be a problem at school, but then she noticed that taking deep breaths helped her shrink her anger at school. She still struggles with anger when she's with her family at home or in shopping centers.

When thinking of ways to start her skills toolbox, Jenny remembered that deep breaths had helped keep her anger from getting out of control at school. These deep breaths reminded Jenny of blowing up a balloon, so she drew a balloon for her toolbox. She made a copy of her drawing to keep with her during the day. Looking at it reminded her to take deep breaths and helped her anger not get so big. Even just feeling her drawing in her pocket helped Jenny think of the balloon, and that reminded her to take deep breaths at home and in shopping centers, too. Jenny started using this tool at school, but now she has been able to use it to keep her anger in control in other places.

For You to Do

Draw a picture of a tool you already have to help you shrink your feelings. You might use that tool only in one place right now, like Jenny first used her deep breaths only at school, and that's okay. Think of other times you notice a big feeling. Could you use your tool during these other times? Make a list under your drawing of everywhere you could use your tool.

BRAKE!

For You to Know

Being aware, or mindful, of your feelings, thoughts, and actions can help you learn to slow down and make better choices in overwhelming moments.

When you are slowing down a car, you have to press the brakes. Feelings can speed up like a car. They can sneak up on you, and they can be big and scary. What can you do when your feelings move fast and feel so big that you just don't know what to do? One thing you can do is BRAKE!

B—Take a deep **breath**. Breathing tells your brain to slow down.

R—**Relax** your muscles—shake 'em out!

A—**Ask** your fact mind to balance out the feelings.

K—Be **kind** to yourself and others with your words and actions.

E—**Enter** the situation when you are ready to make good decisions.

In activity 20, you learned about feelings, urges, and behaviors. Use BRAKE to stop and notice your urge before acting on it. This can help you make better decisions.

For You to Do

Practice using BRAKE in the next few days. Practice first when you are calm and then when you are having a big feeling. Use this chart to check off each part of BRAKE you use, and then write about what happened.

Part of BRAKE You Used	What Happened
__ Take a deep **breath**. __ **Relax** your muscles. __ **Ask** your fact mind. __ Be **kind**. __ **Enter** the situation when you are ready.	
__ Take a deep **breath**. __ **Relax** your muscles. __ **Ask** your fact mind. __ Be **kind**. __ **Enter** the situation when you are ready.	
__ Take a deep **breath**. __ **Relax** your muscles. __ **Ask** your fact mind. __ Be **kind**. __ **Enter** the situation when you are ready.	

When Your Brain Overheats

For You to Know

The amygdala is the part in the center of your brain that is responsible for how you respond to emotions. The frontal lobe is where decision making takes place. These parts have to work together to help you make good choices.

Did you know that the human brain is 75 percent water? Even with that much water, it can overheat at times. When you have a big feeling, blood runs to your amygdala in the center of your brain and away from your frontal lobe. When that happens, your amygdala and frontal lobe are not working together, and it becomes hard to make good decisions.

To get the parts of your brain to work together, try cooling it down. When you are having a big feeling and the parts of your brain are not working together, put something cold on your eyes and face, and hold it there for twenty to thirty seconds. Doing that will help the blood move away from your amygdala and back to your frontal lobe. It's like telling your brain to chill out!

For You to Do

During the next week, practice putting something cool on your face when you have a big, strong feeling. Use the chart below to list the feeling you had, and notice if your feeling went up, down, or stayed the same.

Feeling	What Happened After You Cooled Yourself Down
	__ My feeling went away a little. Cooling down was helpful. __ My feeling stayed the same. Cooling down had no effect. __ My feeling felt bigger. Cooling down was not helpful.
	__ My feeling went away a little. Cooling down was helpful. __ My feeling stayed the same. Cooling down had no effect. __ My feeling felt bigger. Cooling down was not helpful.
	__ My feeling went away a little. Cooling down was helpful. __ My feeling stayed the same. Cooling down had no effect. __ My feeling felt bigger. Cooling down was not helpful.
	__ My feeling went away a little. Cooling down was helpful. __ My feeling stayed the same. Cooling down had no effect. __ My feeling felt bigger. Cooling down was not helpful.
	__ My feeling went away a little. Cooling down was helpful. __ My feeling stayed the same. Cooling down had no effect. __ My feeling felt bigger. Cooling down was not helpful.

Something to think about: Notice if the tool helped your feeling go down and if it helped you make good choices.

For You to Know

Your muscles can tense up when you have strong feelings, and you may not even notice. Tense muscles tell your brain that you are having a big feeling. By learning how to loosen your muscles, you can gain some control over your behaviors and emotions.

Sometimes your mind starts thinking about too many things at once. When this happens, your mind sends messages to your body telling you that you are tense. This makes your muscles stiff, just like uncooked noodles. When you have big feelings, your feelings can also send messages to your body that make you feel stiff and tense.

Guess what? You can learn how to get rid of that stiff, tense feeling in your body by teaching your muscles how to relax. Relaxing your muscles helps slow down your thoughts and shrink your big emotions.

To start, imagine a brand-new box of noodles. Each noodle is stiff, just like your muscles are when they get tense. Practice tensing up your whole body so it is stiff like an uncooked noodle. Try to make your whole body as tall and straight as possible, so stiff that you are not able to bend at all. Remember, you cannot bend a noodle that has not been cooked!

Now, imagine what a noodle looks and feels like after it has been cooked. If you put a bunch of cooked noodles onto a plate, they would be curled up and easy to bend into any shape. They would feel soft. Try to make your whole body as loose as possible, just like a cooked noodle.

The more you practice this, the easier it will be for you to notice when your muscles are tense and when they are relaxed. When you start noticing that you feel tense, you will be able to practice tensing and relaxing, and this will help you gain control over how your body feels by allowing you to relax at any time.

For You to Do

Read this script all the way through before practicing to become familiar with what is being asked. You might find it helpful to record your voice reading the script so that you can focus on your muscles tensing and relaxing while listening to the instructions instead of while reading them. If you don't have a way to record yourself reading this script, ask a friend or trusted adult to read the script to you so you can focus on practicing the actions without having to read the instructions at the same time. To get the hang of this activity you need to practice it over and over.

- Notice the top of your head. Imagine that your hair is a bunch of stiff, uncooked noodles. Now tense up the top of your head so that all those stiff noodles don't break. Then imagine that the noodles begin to relax as they are cooked in hot water. As you imagine this, relax all the muscles that were tense on the top of your head so that your head and hair are loose, just like cooked noodles.

- Notice your face. Imagine that it is stiff like an uncooked noodle. Tense every muscle in your face as much as you can. Then relax those muscles and imagine that they are now loose like soft, cooked noodles.

- Notice your shoulders. Tighten up your shoulders like a stiff noodle. Then loosen your shoulder muscles, and imagine them being soft and relaxed like cooked noodles.

- Notice your arms. Straighten them so they are long and stiff like uncooked noodles. Make them as stiff and straight as you possibly can. Then relax your arms so they are soft and loose like cooked noodles.

- Notice your stomach. Sit up straight, or stand so that you can tighten your stomach muscles as tight and stiff as you can. Then slouch or sit down so your stomach muscles can become soft and loose like cooked noodles.

- Notice your legs. Stretch them out, or stand so you can tighten them to be as stiff and tense as uncooked noodles. Then bend your legs or return to a sitting position, and notice how it feels when your legs become loose like soft, cooked noodles.

- Notice your feet and your toes. Stiffen them up to be as tight as you can. Then relax them while imagining that they are becoming soft and loose like cooked noodles.

DISTRACT

For You to Know

The human brain is wired to focus on negative and stressful events more than on positive and happy events. To change this, you have to retrain your brain to focus on positive thoughts.

Have you ever found that you just could not stop thinking about something that made you upset or sad? You may have noticed that your brain can easily become stuck thinking about negative things or feelings, just like Velcro gets stuck to itself. This doesn't happen only to you; it's something that happens to everyone at times.

When you are having a big feeling, you can change that feeling by distracting your brain with a new thought. When you think about things that make you angry, you can become angrier. When you think about things that make you sad, you can become sadder. You can learn to use what you think about to distract your brain and make it feel a different way. If you are angry and think of something funny, you will laugh and begin to feel happy.

Use the acronym DISTRACT to help you remember all the ways to distract your brain. Keep in mind that you want to distract your brain for short periods of time. Once you are calm and ready to return to the situation that made you upset, go for it!

D—**Do** something else, like a puzzle or playing "I Spy."

I—**Imagine** being somewhere else; for example, in your favorite spot.

S—Tune in to your **senses**: sight, sound, taste, touch, and smell; for example, listen to music or hold your favorite soft toy.

T—**Think** about something else, like your favorite memory.

R—**Read** a book.

A—Do an **art** or craft project.

C—Play a **computer** game.

T—**Try** a new game.

For You to Do

Take a few minutes to brainstorm all of the things you could do to distract your brain when you have big feelings, and write them down here. Remember to share this list with an adult who can help you when your feelings are big.

Do something different:

_____

_____

Imagine being somewhere else:

_____

_____

Tune in to your **senses** (sight, sound, taste, touch, and smell):

_____

_____

Think about something else:

_____

_____

Read a book:

_____

_____

Do **arts** and crafts:

_____

_____

Play a **computer** game:

_____

_____

Try a new game:

_____

_____

> ### *For You to Know*
>
> Taking deep breaths in followed by breathing out really slowly can change the way your body feels. Breathing is a great way to send messages to your brain about what is going on around you. It is also a really helpful tool because you take it with you everywhere you go. You can't forget your breath!

When your brain is anxious, your body naturally begins to take shallow, quick breaths. As your breaths get faster and shorter, your brain starts to feel more anxious because that is the message that shallow, quick breaths send to your brain. They are basically screaming, "Danger!"

You might not always be able to stop this from happening, but you can notice when it does happen. Once you notice that your breaths are short and fast, you can teach yourself how to slow your breathing down. And once your breath slows down, you will notice a change in how you feel. If you can feel your heartbeat in your neck or your chest, you might notice that your heart beats faster when you breathe in and more slowly when you breathe out. When your heartbeat slows down, you feel calmer. This is why focusing on breathing out as slowly as you can is more important than focusing on how deeply you breathe in or how long you hold your breath; it is the slow breathing out that slows your heartbeat and makes your body feel calmer.

It is a good idea to start your breathing practice when you do not have a big feeling so you get a better idea of how it works. This will help you think about breathing as an option when you do have a big feeling. It can be tricky to do this and will take a lot of practice. Just remember, it is possible to slow your breathing, and it works really well once you know how to do it.

For You to Do

Imagine you are a deep-sea diver about to go underwater. You want to fill your lungs with plenty of air, but you also want to slowly go down into the water. Once you have your lungs filled with your deep breath of air, you will very slowly breathe out the air.

Imagine that you slowly go deeper into the water as your breath comes out slowly. Your goal is to go deeper into the water as slowly as possible. Every time you breathe in, it is a chance for you to get fresh air from your air tank. Every time you breathe out slowly, you are getting closer to how you wanted to feel and where you wanted to go, deeply relaxed under the deep, blue sea.

In the space below, draw a picture of yourself breathing like a deep-sea diver. Make big bubbles to show how slowly you are breathing out in order to float deeper into the deep sea of relaxation.

More for You to Do

Now that you have imagined breathing like a deep-sea diver, practice actually breathing deeply and slowly. You will start this practice by breathing in as deeply as you can while you slowly count to 3. (Breathe in 1… 2… 3…)

Now hold that breath for one count and then slowly let it out while counting to 5. (Breathe out 1… 2… 3… 4… 5…) You should have breath coming out slowly all the way until you reach the count of 5.

Pause for a second and start breathing in, slowly and deeply, counting to 3 again. Repeat this three to five times. Then stop, breathe normally, and notice how you feel. Write down what you notice in your body:

_____

_____

_____

You Have to DEAL

> ## *For You to Know*
>
> You don't always get to have things your way, and when things don't go your way, it can be very frustrating. In order to DEAL, you might have to let go of getting your way!

You have been learning about how to change your thoughts and feelings and about ways to check if your feeling fits the facts of the situation. This activity is going to look at putting some of those activities together.

Imagine you are out having fun with your mom and sister. Your sister gets to buy something for herself with her birthday money. Even though you understand that her birthday just happened and yours was a long time ago, you still think it is unfair, and this makes you mad. You remember the pages about feelings in this workbook, and you ask yourself if your anger fits the facts (Hint: look at activity 7), and it does. Now you have a right to be mad, but what are you going to do? You can complain, cry, or even say mean things, but then what would happen?

Here's an idea: BRAKE (breathe, relax your muscles, ask your fact mind, be kind to yourself and others, and enter the situation when you're ready) and think to yourself, *What is more important to me today? Letting my mom know how unfair this feels to me, or continuing to have fun with my mom and sister?*

If you choose to act on your anger, you will likely get in trouble, you will continue to be in an angry mood all day, and your day might even end poorly. If you choose to continue having fun, you will have to be angry for a few minutes until your anger goes away (it will always go away), and then you will be in a good mood again and you will get to do more fun things. You will probably even have an enjoyable rest of your day. Choosing the second option is learning that sometimes you just have to DEAL!

D—Take **deep** breaths.

E—**Examine** your options.

A—**Ask** yourself, *What is most important right now, in this very moment?*

L—**Listen** to your full mind and do your best.

For You to Do

Practice DEAL this week by paying attention to situations where you notice that you want to get your way. Each time you choose to DEAL instead, congratulate yourself by filling out a copy of the certificate on the following page, which you can download at http://www.newharbinger.com/38594. Circle the actions you take to help you remember exactly how you practiced this skill.

DEAL

Congratulations to me! I was faced with a tough decision when

_____

_____

_____

_____

I made a good choice by taking these steps to help me DEAL:

D—Take **deep** breaths.

E—**Examine** my options.

A—**Ask** myself, _What is most important right now, in this very moment?_

L—**Listen** to my full mind and do my best.

Excellent job!

At http://www.newharbinger.com/38594, you can also download a bonus activity called "Ready for Action or Stuck Demanding Your Own Way?"

Section 5

Taking Your Tools on the Road

It can be helpful to make a different toolbox for different events. For example, Darci has a list of songs on her smartphone to listen to when she expects to be in the car for a really long time. This is a skills toolbox she takes with her on long car trips to keep her from being too bored in the car. Paul brings a backpack of comic books with him when he goes to his grandma's house for the weekend because his grandma doesn't have a television, and in the past Paul has struggled with big feelings from not having something to do while staying there. The bag of comic books is Paul's skills toolbox for visits at his grandma's house.

You might have a toolbox of ideas that help in many situations, and those ideas (or tools) can be included in any special toolbox you create. It can also be helpful to make a specific skills toolbox for times when you might need extra reminders of a tool you don't always use. For example, if you know you are going to talk to a friend about something important and that makes you feel anxious, you might have a special skills toolbox just for this occasion.

This section will give you more ideas about how to make a special skills toolbox for special occasions. We used acronyms to create reminders to help you remember the skills. Remember, an acronym is a reminder word formed from the beginning letters of an idea. And keep in mind that your skills toolbox can be anything you want it to be!

Planning Ahead for Big Feelings—PLAN

For You to Know

Worrying about things not going well is like practicing or rehearsing for things not to go well. That becomes all we know, and we might end up doing what we had practiced in our mind. When we plan for coping well, it becomes easier to make that happen.

When you imagine a situation that starts a big feeling for you, do you think of it going well or not going so well? Most people notice thoughts about the situation not going so well. This is normal, but it also tends to make our big feelings get even bigger. Think about all of the skills you have learned in this workbook so far. What skills might help you get through a situation without any big feelings getting in the way? The PLAN acronym can help you with this.

P—Picture yourself controlling a big feeling. What does that look like if you have a big feeling and you handle it well? Is it hard to imagine having a big feeling and controlling your actions? If so, keep practicing imagining what it could look like to have feelings and still be in control.

L—List the tools you imagined using to help you feel in control. These will be important tools to rehearse or practice. Think about the tools you have learned in this book and rehearse them any chance you get. The more you practice using your tools when your feelings are small, the more likely you will be to know how to use your tools when your emotions get big.

A—What **actions** have you done when you had this big feeling in the past? What actions could you do that are helpful and not hurtful? Write down specific actions you want to do and practice actually doing them. It can help to imagine doing these actions when you have a big feeling. That way, you are more likely to do the action you want rather than the action that normally gets you in trouble when you have a big feeling.

N—It's easy to put things off until later, but right **now** is the time to practice using helpful tools and rehearsing helpful actions. The more you practice using your tools and acting in helpful ways right now, in this very moment, the easier it will be to do these things when a big feeling pops up. It could help to rehearse or practice this with an adult you trust. Ask questions and be open to feedback.

For You to Do

Think of a situation where you would normally have a big feeling. Now, write out a plan for what that situation might look like when you use your skills to cope well.

P—Picture yourself controlling a big feeling. What does that look like if you have a big feeling and you handle it well?

_____

_____

_____

L—List the tools you imagined using that help you feel in control, and write down how you can rehearse each:

_____

_____

_____

A—Write down specific **actions** you want to do and practice actually doing these actions:

_____

_____

_____

Don't Let Your Emotions Run Your Life for Kids

N—Make a plan or schedule for practicing **now**:

_____

_____

_____

After you rehearse your plan and use it, write down what you noticed. Did it go well? Why or why not? If you could do something differently, what would you do? This will be something to share with an adult so you can get ideas of what helped and what didn't help.

_____

_____

_____

_____

_____

Getting What You Need from Others—PLEASE

For You to Know

Interacting with other people can be hard and can bring up a lot of different thoughts and feelings. Many kids find it hard to ask for the things they need when they are having a lot of big feelings. Their feelings can sometimes get in the way.

When you have to ask for something, it can help to think ahead about what you are going to say. You've probably heard people say that it is important to say please when you ask for something. PLEASE can also be a useful tool to help you plan exactly what to say.

P—Pick a good time. Think about how other people are feeling before you decide to ask. Are they busy doing a lot of things? Do they look like they are in good moods? If people are in bad moods when you ask for something and they say no, it might be because they are having some uncomfortable thoughts and feelings. When that happens, you need to wait for them to be ready to talk to you.

L—List the facts of the situation. Begin by listing the facts before asking for what you need. Giving other people the facts will help them to know more about why you are asking.

E—Express how you feel about the situation. Once you have listed the facts, you can share with the person how you feel about those facts and about the situation.

A—Ask for what you need. Now is the time to go ahead and ask the other person for what you need. Be sure to be honest and say it in a way that the person can understand exactly what it is you are asking for.

S—Stay calm! Remember to use your tools from this book. The other person might say no to your request. If this happens, it is important to stay calm. Remember to use your breathing skills.

E—End your request with a statement about how this conversation felt. Did you get what you wanted? Great! Tell the person how nice it feels that he or she gave you what you asked for. It can still be helpful to tell someone how you feel even if you did not get what you asked for or if it didn't go so well. Saying "I understand that I can't have this now. It's really important to me and I'm sad, but I do understand" is a nice way to take a "No" while still telling someone how you feel. If a conversation isn't going well, you might say, "This doesn't seem like a good time to talk. I'm going to take a break for now. Let's talk about this later when we are both calm."

For You to Do

Think of a situation where you have something you want to ask for. Use the PLEASE tool you just learned and the outline below to make a plan for asking.

What exactly is it you are asking for? What is your goal? Write it out clearly.

P—Pick a good time. Write down ideas of when you think it would be a good time to ask.

_____

_____

_____

L—List the facts of the situation.

_____

_____

_____

E—Express how you feel about the situation.

_____

_____

_____

A—**Ask** for what you need.

_____

_____

_____

S—**Stay** calm! List the tools you will use to help yourself stay calm.

_____

_____

_____

E—**End** your request with a statement about how this conversation felt.

_____

_____

_____

Nurturing Relationships with Others—CARE

For You to Know

It is important to show others that you care about them if you want them to show that they care about you. This is how we build friendships.

It can be hard to show other people that you care about them when your feelings tell you someone has been mean or just doesn't care. It might be true that someone is actually just mean or just doesn't care. If you think this is the case, ask yourself, *How do I know this person is mean or doesn't care?* If you have a hard time answering that question with facts, it might be that your feelings are getting in the way.

You can use the acronym CARE to help you think about how to care about someone.

C—Be curious. When you are curious about people, you look at them as if you have never seen them before. If you are meeting someone for the very first time, you might be curious about what his name is, what he likes to do for fun, or whether he plays any sports. You don't assume you know something just by looking at a person. For example, if someone has her arms crossed, lips pressed together, and eyebrows tensed while staring at you (like she might be mad at you), you might be curious and say to her, "I'm noticing your arms are crossed, and you're looking toward me like you might be mad at me. Are you mad at me?" If the person *is* mad at you, she could tell you that. And if she *is not* mad at you, she could tell you that. If you are curious, you will be open to hearing what the person has to say.

A—Ask questions, and don't assume you already know the answers. Your feelings can sometimes get in the way of seeing the facts. This is why it is really important to ask questions. For example, let's say you can't find your favorite pen,

Don't Let Your Emotions Run Your Life for Kids

and then you see your friend Ben writing with it. The facts are that Ben has your pen and he is writing with it. If you assume he took your pen without asking, you might get really angry with Ben. You could ask Ben if he knows that he is using your pen, because he might not know it is yours. If Ben tells you he knows it is your pen, you could ask, "Why did you take my pen without asking?" That way you could hear what Ben has to say before assuming he did something mean on purpose. Maybe Ben was in a hurry to write something down and just grabbed the first pen he saw without thinking. You might not be too mad at Ben if you hear his explanation.

R—Really listen to what you hear, and repeat it back to make sure you heard everything that was said. Now is not the time to say whether you agree or disagree. It can be more important just to show that you are really listening.

You don't just want to repeat every word you hear! For example, if your mom asks you to clean your room and you repeat back, "Clean your room, clean your room," it might seem like you are being mean, and that's not what CARE is about. Try to repeat back a feeling or repeat something you think sounds important. For example, if someone says, "I'm just so frustrated!" you can repeat back, "You sound frustrated." That's it!

E—Express understanding. When you express understanding, you try to find something that you really do understand. You can tell others that you understand their feelings without agreeing with their actions. This can be really hard to do if you do not agree with what a person did. Remember, you are looking for something that you *do* understand when you practice CARE. For example, if Ben was angry about getting a bad grade and yelled at you, you might be able to understand that he was angry. Understanding that does not mean you have to agree with the fact that he yelled at you. It just means you understand what it is like to be angry.

For You to Do

Make a plan for how you can show that you care for someone.

C—Remember, when you are **curious** about someone, you look for facts that tell you someone really cares and you don't *only* pay attention to your feelings. What would it look like if you were curious about someone? Write some ideas here:

_____

_____

_____

Think of some times when it would be helpful to be curious about a situation. List your examples here:

_____

_____

_____

A—**Ask** questions and do not assume you already know the answers. Have your feelings ever gotten in the way of seeing the facts? Write down an example here:

_____

_____

_____

What questions could you ask to help you know the facts? List some questions you could ask here:

_____

_____

_____

R—Really listen to what you hear and repeat it back to make sure you heard everything that was said. Write down some examples here of what you said when repeating back what you heard:

_____

_____

_____

E—Express understanding. For example, you could say, "It sounds like you had a really busy day. It makes sense that you're feeling tired." Write down some other examples here of what you can say to express understanding:

_____

_____

_____

Setting Limits with Others—HALT

For You to Know

When you set limits with others, you teach them how to treat you in a way that you want to be treated.

Have you ever felt frustrated, sad, or anxious because it seemed like someone was not treating you the way you want to be treated? It can really help to notice the facts about what happened, and your feelings about those facts, when someone treats you in a way you do not like. This can help you tell people exactly what you wish they would do differently in the future.

For example, let's pretend you are friends with Jane. Jane often yells, "Get over here!" when she wants you to play with her or when she wants you to do something that *she* wants to do. What are the facts? Jane does not ask if you want to play; she says, "Get over here" in a loud voice. What are your feelings about those facts? Different people would have different feelings. Let's just pretend you have a thought that says *Jane is bossing me around,* and that starts an angry feeling.

Stop to think about what your goal might be in this situation. Your goal might be that Jane ask you if you want to play rather than tell you to "get over here." Your goal might be that Jane not use such a loud voice when talking to you.

You can use the acronym HALT to help you tell Jane how you want to be treated. By telling Jane what you like and do not like, you have helped her know what to do differently. You are teaching Jane how to treat you. Jane can, of course, decide not to listen. You cannot control whether Jane does what you ask, but that does not mean you shouldn't try to tell her how you want her to treat you. Who knows? Maybe Jane did not realize how loud she was, and maybe she did not know that it makes you angry when she tells you what to do instead of asking. If you tell her, she might change these things, and you can feel proud because you stood up for yourself.

H—Have a goal when speaking to someone, and stick to that goal. Did someone hurt your feelings? Is your goal to ask someone not to hurt your feelings? Make sure you can describe the facts or behaviors and words you noticed that led to your hurt feelings.

Example: Jane yelled at you and called you stupid when you did not answer her questions right away. Your goal might be to tell Jane not to call you names and to please not yell.

A—Ask for what you want or state what you need directly. Be specific.

Example: "Jane, please don't speak to me so loudly and don't call me names."

L—Look the person you are talking to in the eyes. Stand tall and proud. Saying something positive silently to yourself can help you feel more confident. Think of statements that might help you.

Example: *It's okay to stand up for myself,* or *I got this,* or *If I don't tell Jane to stop, it doesn't make sense to expect that she will stop. It's important to tell her how I want to be treated.*

T—Take deep breaths, and keep your muscles as relaxed as possible. When you stand tall with relaxed muscles you appear confident to others, and you are less likely to have a big feeling take control. It might help to review the script for activity 27 ("Relaxing Your Muscles") and activity 29 ("Deep Breathing"). Take a moment to practice those skills before you set your limit.

For You to Do

Think of a time when you had a big feeling after someone said or did something you didn't like. Write your own script using HALT to set a limit with that person. Practice this, and imagine what it would look like if it went well. After rehearsing it a few times, you can use the script you practiced to see if it helps you set a limit with someone.

H—Have a goal when speaking to someone and stick to that goal. Write down an example of a goal you have:

_____

_____

A—Ask for what you want or state what you need directly. Be specific. Write down what facts you want the person to change:

_____

_____

L—Look the person you are talking to in the eyes. List some positive self-statements to help you feel confident:

_____

_____

T—Take deep breaths, and keep your muscles as relaxed as possible. Practice thinking of breathing when it would normally be hard to be confident. Write down things you noticed in yourself after practicing your breathing:

_____

_____

For You to Know

Your imagination can be an amazing tool! Imagining that you have a superpower might not turn you into a real-life superhero, but it can help you feel more powerful and more in control.

For this activity you are going to imagine that you are a feelings superhero. You can be any kind of feelings superhero that you want. The trick is, your feelings superhero self needs to be completely in control of your feelings.

Some feelings superheroes can do amazing things. For instance, Super Sammy has a sad-zapper that can zap mean words so they can't hurt him so much. When someone says mean things to Sammy, things that might make his sadness really big, Super Sammy's sad-zapper comes out and zaps those hurtful words so they cannot get to Sammy.

Invincible Isaac is another feelings superhero. Invincible Isaac has a special invisible protection bubble that protects him when there is a strong storm. Isaac used to have a really big feeling of fear when there was a thunderstorm, but now Invincible Isaac comes out to save the day every time a storm approaches. By popping up his invisible protection bubble at the first sound of thunder, Invincible Isaac is able to remember that he is safe from the storm. The storm can't get past the protection bubble. It's pretty amazing!

Caitlyn Cool is a feelings superhero, too. Caitlyn Cool reminds Caitlyn how to take deep, slow breaths to get calm and cool when something makes her feel really angry. Caitlyn Cool has supercool sunglasses and a supershady umbrella that blocks out anger. When anger gets big, it is like a really hot sunny day. If Caitlyn hangs out in the shade of Caitlyn Cool's umbrella with her supersunglasses on, she can still notice that it is sunny, but she won't get too hot and the sun cannot burn her. With anger, like the sun, sometimes it helps to have a "shady" place to take a break so you do not get "too hot" or do something that gets you in trouble.

It can be helpful to think of yourself as a feelings superhero with the ability to use superpowers to control your feelings, because believing you can control your feelings actually does help you control them sometimes. Remember, controlling your feelings does not mean you have to completely ignore them. Caitlyn Cool can still notice the sun, but it is easier to notice it when she is in the shade and not getting a sunburn. You can still notice your feelings, too. Just think of your superpower as something helpful that keeps you in control of what you say or do.

For You to Do

In order to be completely in control of your feelings, you must have some pretty cool superpowers. What kind of superpowers would you have if you could have any superpower in the world? Remember, your superpower needs to be something that can control your biggest feelings. Write down some of your ideas here:

_____

_____

_____

_____

On the next page, draw your superhero self. What do your superpowers look like? Try to draw that too! This drawing can be helpful to keep with you when you go somewhere or do something that brings up big feelings for you. If you have a hard time thinking of your superhero self, use this picture as a reminder. You might consider hanging your superhero drawing up in your room where you can be reminded of all you can do.

Don't Let Your Emotions Run Your Life for Kids

Section 6

Values and Goals

In this section, you will learn about your values and goals and how to achieve them. In other words, you will focus on what is important to you. As you go through this section, keep in mind that these can be difficult ideas to understand and you may need an adult to help you. That is okay. Even some adults are not sure what their values and goals are.

This section also helps you learn how to set goals and break them down into smaller, more achievable steps. Sometimes having a goal can be overwhelming, and you might be tempted to give up because it looks too big to accomplish. The activities in this section are meant to help with this.

What Are Your Values?

For You to Know

You can learn about values by watching how the people you look up to act in the world. How do they treat their friends? What do they think about their jobs? How do they look at jobs or chores around the house? All these things will help you know what is important to them.

Values are things you think are important. You might be thinking of actual things, like your bike or a favorite stuffed animal or book, but values are things you cannot always see. Values are behaviors or beliefs that you follow as you go through each day. They are sometimes referred to as virtues.

Let's take the value of honesty as an example. If you value honesty, you do not lie to people you interact with, and you do your best to always be honest. When you stick to your values, you feel good about yourself and build up positive thoughts and feelings about yourself.

It will be helpful for you to take some time to think about what you value. This will help you create goals and think about the kind of person you want to be.

For You to Do

Look at the list of values on the following page. For each one, write down how you define the value and then how it looks when you put it into action through your behaviors. The first two have been completed as examples.

Some of these words might be new to you. If so, take the time to look them up. When you are all done, circle the ones that are the most important to you. Add some of your own, if you can think of others.

Value	Definition	What It Looks Like in Action
Honesty	*Telling the truth*	*Do not lie when you talk with others. Do not steal. Pay for things you want or need.*
Learning	*Being curious and interested in things*	*Try reading a new book. Try a new food or game.*
Empathy		
Thankfulness		
Kindness		
Respect		
Imagination		
Hard work		
Perseverance		
Friendship		

Don't Let Your Emotions Run Your Life for Kids

For You to Know

Knowing your values leads to setting goals. Values that are important to you help you decide what your goals are because your goals will be like steps that take you closer to your values.

Goals are things that you want and are working on getting. Some goals are short term and some are long term. Short-term goals are things you want to achieve in the next day or near future. For example, you might have a short-term goal of getting a 100 percent on your next spelling test. Long-term goals are things you want to achieve that will take a little extra work, like getting an A in spelling for the year. Long-term goals often involve a few steps, or short-term goals. Both kinds of goals are important.

Let's say you decide you want the newest Lego set. You have the value of hard work and the goal of getting the new Lego set. How are these things connected? You can choose to keep asking your mom for the Lego set, or you can choose to use your value of hard work by doing extra chores for money and saving your money until you can buy the Lego set all on your own. As you do extra chores each week, you are reaching your short-term goal of saving money. When you have enough money to buy the Lego set, you have reached your long-term goal, and you have done this by thinking about your value of hard work.

Imagine that you do it and you get the Lego set all on your own! How would you feel about yourself after achieving this goal? How important would that Lego set be after you work hard and pay for it yourself?

For You to Do

Review the values you circled as important in activity 36. Think about these, and write down some short-term and long-term goals on the lines below. For example, if you choose the value of friendship, you could start by asking yourself, *What can I do tomorrow at school that will make me a good friend?* Your short-term goal could be to ask a certain person to play tomorrow at recess, and your long-term goal could be to make more friends this year.

Value: _____

Short-term goal: _____

_____

Long-term goal: _____

_____

Value: _____

Short-term goal: _____

_____

Long-term goal: _____

_____

For You to Know

Your goals are like mountains. Some are big and some are small. The first step to reaching your goals is to figure out what they are, and the next is to make a step-by-step plan for reaching them. Then you can start climbing your mountains!

Imagine your values are like clouds in the sky. Just like the clouds, you can never actually grab a value and say, "I've reached it! I don't have to work on this ever again!" Values are things you are working on all the time. Values tell you about the kind of person you want to be. Your values help you set goals. You will tend to feel happy when you are working on goals that match your values.

Sample Values

Honesty

Kindness

Helpfulness

Hard Work

Now imagine that your goals are like mountains. Just like a mountaintop, you can actually reach a goal. When you have a big goal, it is like climbing a big mountain; it will take longer to reach the top. It is important to remember that not all big goals are impossible; some just take more work than others do. You need tools to climb a mountain, just as you need tools to reach your goals. The tools needed to climb a mountain will be different depending on the mountain, just as the tools you use and the steps you take to reach your goals will be different depending on your values and your goals.

Sample Goals

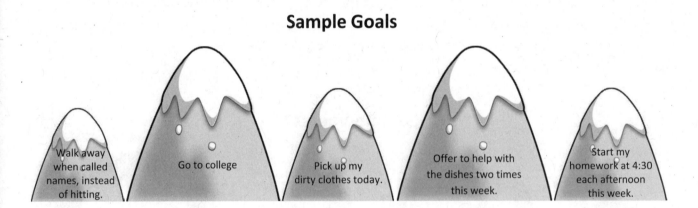

Walk away when called names, instead of hitting.

Go to college

Pick up my dirty clothes today.

Offer to help with the dishes two times this week.

Start my homework at 4:30 each afternoon this week.

For You to Do

List a few of your values in the clouds below.

List some of your goals on the mountains below. Are you working on these goals now, or do you want to work on them in the future? Do you know what tools you need to work on these goals? Take the first step toward one of your goals today!

Ask yourself, *What makes it hard to reach these goals?* For example, it can seem too hard to reach a goal if the first step seems too big or too far away. Try to think of smaller steps. Think of something you can do right now that would be a small step toward a bigger goal.

You'll find two helpful bonus activities—"Setting SMART Goals" and "Activate to Regulate: Every Step Counts"—at http://www.newharbinger.com/38594.

Write down some small steps for a goal you listed:

_____

_____

_____

What tools do you need to help you reach this goal?

_____

_____

_____

People Have Different Values and Goals

For You to Know

A judgment is a decision or conclusion about a situation. Two different people can have two different opinions about something being good or bad, and that does not mean one person is right and one person is wrong. They just have different opinions, and that's okay.

Imagine you are a tiny mouse just minding your own business when suddenly a huge cat comes chasing after you. As the tiny mouse, you might be thinking, *Help! That huge cat is going to get me! I am so scared! Whatever will I do! This is so bad!*

Now, imagine that instead of being the mouse, you are the cat. How would you feel and think? You might feel good and think, *Yippee! This is the best! I haven't had this much fun all day! I am sooo superhungry! I hope I catch that tiny mouse snack soon. Better hurry up and get 'em!*

Notice that if you check with our friend, Frankie Fact from activity 2, he would tell you that the facts of the story have not changed. The facts are there is a mouse, there is a cat, the mouse is running, the cat is running, and the cat is hungry. Fiona Feeling from activity 2 would tell you how both the cat and the mouse have different feelings about the situation.

As soon as you think of the cat as bad or the mouse as good, you are judging or making a decision about who is the good guy and who is the bad guy. Think about that for a moment. The cat is just hungry; that is understandable. You have been hungry before; does that make you a bad guy? The mouse does not want to be the cat's dinner; that also makes sense. When you remove your judgments (good or bad) from the story, you can understand the thoughts of both the cat and the mouse.

This same thing can happen when people have different values and goals. Sometimes you are quick to decide if they are good or bad. What if they were just different? They do not always have to be good or bad.

Have you ever thought of yourself as good or bad? Do those thoughts help you? It could be that you are just the way you are, and that is different from someone else. It doesn't have to be good or bad.

For You to Do

Accepting that different people have different views, values, and goals may be a hard thing for you to notice and change. Many adults have a difficult time with this, and they have been practicing for years. Try the following two exercises to practice this way of thinking.

Imagine a person you have a disagreement with; for example, a friend you were mad at or a sibling who used your things without asking. Imagine understanding why that person feels or thinks the way he or she does. Write down your ideas here:

_____

_____

_____

Practice describing your day by listing just the facts, like the ones you just read about in the cat-and-mouse story. Notice how hard it is to not describe things as good or bad, right or wrong. Write down what you notice about this here:

_____

_____

_____

_____

A Note of Congratulations

Congratulations! You have done a lot of hard work. Please continue to use the tools you learned throughout this workbook to maintain control over your feelings, thoughts, and behaviors. Fill out the certificate on the following page (or download a copy at http://www.newharbinger.com/38594) and keep it displayed somewhere as a reminder for yourself that your emotions don't have to run your life. You have the power to take control for YOU!

This Certificate of Achievement is awarded to

_____

For completing Don't Let Your Emotions Run
Your Life for Kids

On _____

(date of completion)

Additional Resources

Anxiety and Depression

Beck, J. 2011. *Cognitive Behavioral Therapy Basics and Beyond*. 2nd ed. New York: The Guilford Press.

Burns, D. D. 1999. *Feeling Good: The New Mood Therapy*. Revised. New York: Avon Books.

Goldfried, M. R., M. M. Linehan, and J. L. Smith. 1978. "The Reduction of Test Anxiety Through Cognitive Restructuring." *Journal of Consulting and Clinical Psychology* 79: 32–39.

Child Development and Risk Factors for Aggressive Behavior

DeHart, G. B., L. A. Sroufe, and R. G. Cooper. 2004. *Child Development: Its Nature and Course*. 5th ed. New York: McGraw-Hill.

Harachi, T. W., C. B. Fleming, H. R. White, M. E. Ensminger, R. D. Abbot, R. F. Catalono, and K. P. Haggerty. 2006. "Aggressive Behavior Among Girls and Boys During Middle Childhood: Predictors and Sequelae of Trajectory Group Membership." *Aggressive Behavior* 32: 279–293.

Honig, A. S. 1984. "Risk Factors in Infancy." *Early Child Development and Care* 16: 1–8.

Sroufe, L. A., B. Egeland, E. A. Carlson, and W. A. Collins. 2005. *The Development of the Person: The Minnesota Study of Risk and Adaptation from Birth to Adulthood*. New York: The Guilford Press.

Vosniadou, S. 2003. "How Children Learn." In *Successful Schooling*, edited by D. B. Rao. New Delhi: Discovery Publishing House.

Dialectical Behavior Therapy (DBT)

Linehan, M. M. 1993. *Cognitive-Behavioral Treatment of Borderline Personality Disorder.* New York: The Guilford Press.

Linehan, M. M. 1993. *Skills Training Manual for Treating Borderline Personality Disorder.* New York: The Guilford Press.

Linehan, M. M., M. R. Goldfried, and A. P. Goldfried. 1979. "Assertion Therapy: Skill Training or Cognitive Restructuring?" *Behavior Therapy* 10: 372–388.

Rathus, J. H., and A. L. Miller. 2000. "DBT for Adolescents: Dialectical Dilemmas and Secondary Treatment Targets." *Cognitive and Behavioral Practice* 7: 425–434.

Mindfulness

Hayes, A. M., and G. Feldman. 2004. "Clarifying the Construct of Mindfulness in the Context of Emotion Regulation and the Process of Change in Therapy." *Clinical Psychology: Science and Practice* 11: 255–262.

Muth, J. J. 2005. *Zen Shorts.* New York: Scholastic Press.

Nhat Hanh, Thich. 2007. *Planting Seeds: Practicing Mindfulness with Children.* Berkeley, CA: Parallax Press.

Physical Health: Sleep and Fitness

National Sleep Foundation. 2017. "Children and Sleep." n.d. https://sleepfoundation.org/sleep-topics/children-and-sleep.

The Nemours Foundation. 1995–2017). "Fitness and Your 6- to 12-Year-Old." n.d. http://kidshealth.org/en/parents/fitness-6–12.html

Don't Let Your Emotions Run Your Life for Kids

Jennifer J. Solin, PsyD, is a licensed psychologist in private practice in St. Paul, MN. She has over ten years of experience working primarily with children and families, and six years of experience working primarily with adolescents and adults. Psychological services that Solin specializes in include: behavioral therapy (BT), cognitive behavioral therapy (CBT), exposure and ritual/response prevention (EX/RP), prolonged exposure (PE), dialectical behavior therapy (DBT), individual therapy, and group skills training. Solin also supervises graduate students, postdoctoral fellows, and mental health practitioners, and has presented in various conferences, in addition to having provided didactic trainings to medical and mental health staff at local hospitals in the Twin Cities area of Minnesota.

Christina L. Kress, MSW, is a licensed clinical social worker in private practice in St. Paul, MN. Kress has over twelve years of experience treating young children with play therapy and CBT, along with over four years' experience treating adults using DBT. Kress presents annually at the Minnesota Association for Child and Adolescent Mental Health Conference, has been a guest lecturer at St. Catherine's University in St. Paul, MN, and provides clinical supervision to mental health practitioners through her practice.

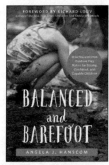
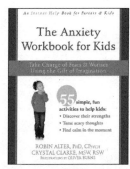

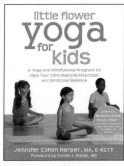

Register your **new harbinger** titles for additional benefits!

When you register your **new harbinger** title—purchased in any format, from any source—you get access to benefits like the following:

- Downloadable accessories like printable worksheets and extra content

- Instructional videos and audio files

- Information about updates, corrections, and new editions

Not every title has accessories, but we're adding new material all the time.

Access free accessories in 3 easy steps:

1. Sign in at NewHarbinger.com (or **register** to create an account).

2. Click on **register a book**. Search for your title and click the **register** button when it appears.

3. Click on the **book cover or title** to go to its details page. Click on **accessories** to view and access files.

That's all there is to it!

If you need help, visit:

NewHarbinger.com/accessories

new harbinger
CELEBRATING
40 YEARS